National Curriculum W

Tudor Wales

Contents

1.	Henry Tudor	3
2.	Tudor Wales	7
3.	Rhys ap Gruffydd	13
4.	Law and Order	15
5.	The Protestant Reformation in Wales	20
6.	Union of England and Wales	23
7.	The Dissolution of the Monasteries in Wales	30
8.	Protestants and Catholics	37
9.	The Welsh Bible	41
10.	Elizabethan Wales	48
	Glossary	55
	Welsh Tudor Biographies	58

A Note on Money

Sums have been given throughout the book in pre-decimal currency in which there were twelve pence (12d) to a shilling (1s) and twenty shillings to a pound (£1).

In 1550 a skilled craftsman was earning about 3p a day. Whereas a farm labourer received half this sum. The gap between the income of most people and the large land-owners was extremely large. Whereas in the 1520s a farm labourer in Wales would earn about £4.50 a year, Thomas Wolsey had an annual income of £50,000.

Comparisons of prices are difficult because people today can buy very different things from those available to people during the Tudor period. However, the price of basic foodstuffs give us some guide to the changes that have taken place. A loaf of bread in 1540 cost about 0.5p, which was about a half of the labourer's daily wage.

1. Henry Tudor

On 22 August, 1485, Henry Tudor defeated Richard III at the battle of Bosworth Field. Richard III was killed in the battle and Henry became King of England. The people of Wales hoped that they would benefit from the reign of Henry VII.

Henry Tudor had relied heavily on the support of important Welsh landowners such as Rhys ap Thomas and Sir William Stanley to help defeat Richard III. It has been claimed that over a third of Henry's soldiers at Bosworth had come from Wales. Many historians believe that Henry Tudor would not have been able to seize the throne without the support of the Welsh.

After becoming king, Henry rewarded his Welsh supporters. Jasper Tudor, the Earl of Pembroke, who had been chiefly responsible for organising Henry's military campaign, became Justiciar of Wales and Lord of Glamorgan.

Rhys ap Thomas was knighted and became Chamberlain of Carmarthen and Cardigan. Thomas was also appointed Chief Justice of South Wales and Sir William Stanley was awarded the posts of Chamberlain of the Royal Household and Chief Justice of North Wales.

---

(1) Poem written by Lewys Glyn Cothi in 1485
Jasper, what preparations do you make?
In what seas are your anchors?
When, O black bull, will you turn to land?
How long shall we have to wait?

(2) David Powell, *The History of Cambria* (1584)
King Henry VII, who by his grandfather Owen Tudor descended out of Wales... granted them a charter of liberties, whereby they were released from that oppression.

(3) A portrait of Henry VII painted by Michael Sittow in 1505.

(4) C. S. Davies, *The Tudors* (1969)
No less than thirty-five bards apparently produced verses for the Tudor cause. Henry Tudor, of course, was not in any meaningful sense a Welshman, although his grandfather, Owen had been... Once established on the English throne, Henry had no reason to please the Welsh. .. Little was done for the Welsh people, although numbers of individual Welshman made a career for themselves at court.

Welshmen who had taken part in the battle were rewarded with important positions, such as sheriffs, constables, coroners, woodwards and bailiffs. Welshmen were also appointed to public office in London. Henry's physician, usher, sergeant of the guard and most of his personal bodyguard came from Wales. Welsh poets and musicians were also recruited to entertain Henry at his court.

Henry VII also arranged for Welshmen to obtain senior positions in the Church. The most important of these was John Morgan who in 1496 was the first Welshman in over a hundred years to become Bishop of St Davids.

Despite the preferment of Welshmen, many Welsh people felt betrayed by Henry VII. When he was recruiting soldiers in Wales before the Battle of Bosworth, Henry had criticised the way the Welsh people had been treated in the past by English monarchs and promised to bring an end to their "miserable servitude". During the first twenty years of his reign, Henry VII did little to improve the life of ordinary people living in Wales.

It was not until 1505 that Henry VII began issuing charters in Wales which removed the last remaining aspects of the feudal system. Two years later Henry VII issued a proclamation that granted Welsh people the same legal rights as people living in England. Conversely, Englishmen who broke the law in Wales could now be tried before a Welsh jury.

(5) Andreas Trevisano, Venetian ambassador (1497)
The Welsh may now be said to have recovered their former independence, for the most wise and fortunate Henry VII is a Welshman.

(6) Michael Alexander, *The First of the Tudors* (1981)
Henry Tudor's triumph at Bosworth was considered a victory for Wales also; and shortly after 1485 scores of ambitious Welshmen crossed the border into England... Before 1485 the main positions in the Welsh church had always gone to Englishmen, a practice that now ceased. Not only did Henry VII appoint Welshmen to the four bishoprics in their native land, but also selected them for important positions in both England and Ireland.

(7) Christopher Morris, *The Tudors*, (1955)
Henry Tudor... was consciously aware of being Welsh. Fourteen of the first twenty-eight years of his life had been spent on Welsh soil. He rewarded Welsh bards and kept St David's Day. He called his eldest son after King Arthur. He used the red dragon of Cadwallader as supporter for the royal arms and had flown it as the royal standard on the field of Bosworth.

1.1 Read sources 2, 4, 6, 7 and the biography of Henry Tudor on page 64. Explain why many people in Wales considered Henry Tudor to be a Welshman.

1.2 Explain the different ways that Welsh people helped Henry Tudor to become king. You will need to read the text and the sources before answering this question.

1.3 Describe the various ways by which Henry VII rewarded the Welsh people for the support they gave him during his struggle with Richard III.

2. Tudor Wales

It has been estimated that about 250,000 people were living in Wales in 1500. Approximately 85% of the population lived in the southern lowlands and the Welsh lands bordering England. In these fertile areas farmers were able to grow crops of wheat, barley and oats.

In the upland areas, arable farming was much more difficult and so hill farmers concentrated on rearing cattle and sheep. Animals at this time were small when compared to modern animals. On average, Tudor cows were only a quarter of the weight of a modern cow. Cows in the sixteenth century yielded only a sixth of the milk produced by a cow today.

(8) **A drawing of a village in about 1500.**

(9) Frank Emery, *The Farming Regions of Wales, 1500-1640* (1967)
About 58% of Wales is higher than 500 feet above the sea... uplands suffer from heavy rainfall, cloudy skies, and mists, from scant sunshine... boisterous winds, frosts, and blizzards... the hill-farmer has always had to face unremittingly hard labour and meagre returns.

(10) Bernardino de Mendoza, Spanish ambassador in Britain, letter to Philip II of Spain (1586)
Wales is very mountainous, but still very rich in cattle and sheep; there is plenty of wheat.

Sheep owned by Welsh farmers were also small and their wool was coarse and could only be used to make a poor quality cloth. Goats were also kept for their milk, which was used to make butter and cheese.

In Tudor Wales, transporting goods was very expensive. Most farmers living in mountainous areas could not afford to pay the price of imported corn and therefore had to find land to grow crops.

Wales had a small number of yeoman who owned between 30 and 50 acres. However, the vast majority of Welsh farmers owned less than ten acres of land. In many cases, this land did not provide enough food to feed a family and the farmers had to find other work to supplement their income. Some worked part-time as labourers for the larger landowners, while others produced cloth, leather and dairy products which they sold at the local market.

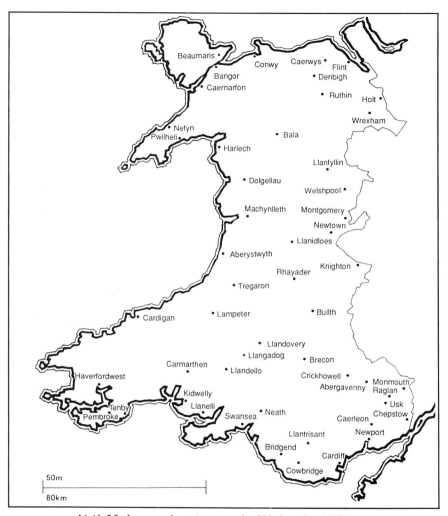

(11) Main market towns in Wales in 1550

(12) E. Lhuyd, *Geographical Dictionary of Wales* (1696)
Between Tregaron and Builth it was.. for the most part
mountainous, rocky, barren; but breeds plenty of good
sheep... In mountainous areas the farmers... fallow the
land... by tying the cattle to stakes on it.

Those who could not find alternative employment had to seek charity from their more prosperous neighbours. After a poor harvest poverty became a major problem and there was always the danger that farmers and their families would suffer malnutrition or face starvation.

The type of house that people lived in depended on their wealth and the region in which they lived. Where timber was available, a wooden frame was built. The Welsh favoured the cruck method where curved timbers, meeting at the centre, supported both the walls and the roof. The walls, often made of a mixture of clay and straw, were only four or five feet high whereas the roof was steep and thatched.

Most houses only had two rooms, one for living and one for sleeping. A fire burned on an open hearth in the middle of the living room, and the smoke found its way out through an opening in the roof. Only the most prosperous farmers lived in houses large enough to have a kitchen. In many cases, people and animals lived under the same roof. Very few people had houses with windows and chimneys. Even as late as 1773 a traveller observed that a large number of houses in Wales were "destitute of chimneys".

---

(13) George Owen, *Description of Pembrokeshire* (1603)
The commodity of corn is the chiefest that bringeth in money to the country... the soil being naturally dry and fit for plough work... The trade of breeding cattle is used much in all parts... but most near the mountains, where the land is not so good for corn.

(14) Tudor Yeoman's House in Llanarth, Monmouthshire

For most people living in Tudor Wales the staple food was bread. One visitor complained that in some villages the only food available was "black, thick, tough oatbread". Vegetables such as peas, beans, onions and leeks were also grown. The majority of people in Wales could rarely afford to eat meat.

A shortage of nutritious food combined with damp and overcrowded homes, made the poor vulnerable to infectious diseases. Children were particularly at risk and it has been estimated that 50% of babies born in Wales died before they reached their first birthday.

Only a small percentage of Welsh people lived in towns. Although there were officially over a hundred towns in Tudor Wales, only half of these were large enough to hold weekly markets. Even the largest towns, such as Carmarthen and Brecon, had populations of less than 2,000 people.

(15) G. Dyfnallt Owen, *Elizabethan Wales* (1962)
For the richer yeoman... meat had become a common dish, and mutton, veal, beef, pork, calves' feet and bacon appeared regularly on their tables... there was no lack of vegetables such as onions, parsnips and beans. Meals were usually washed down with beer or bragot - mulled ale sweetened and spiced - and sour milk. The poorer class of labourers lived on a meagre and often improvised diet. A breast of mutton boiled in porridge was a delicacy for them.

(16) William Harrison, *Description of England* (1577)
Very little food is grown in Wales... the people live idly, dissolutely, and by robbing and stealing from one another.

(17) William Camden, *Britannia* (1586)
The diligence and industry of the Welsh husbandman hath long since begun to conquer the barrenness of the land.

2.1 Study source 8. Describe the various activities that are taking place in this picture.

2.2 Give as many reasons as you can why about 50% of babies born in Tudor Wales died before they reached their first birthday. Select information from the sources to explain why the children of yeoman families were more likely to live longer than children of farmers who owned less than ten acres of land.

2.3 What does source 11 tell you about the people of Wales in 1550? Use information from other sources in this chapter to explain why people decided to live where they did in Tudor Wales.

2.4 Compare the views of William Harrison and William Camden (sources 16 and 17). Give possible reasons why these two men held different opinions on the Welsh people.

3. Rhys ap Gruffydd

In 1525, Rhys ap Thomas, the most important landowner in south-west Wales died. His land was inherited by his grandson Rhys ap Gruffydd. However, Henry VIII, who had replaced his father as king in 1509, was unwilling to allow Rhys ap Gruffydd to inherit the public offices held by his grandfather. The very important post of Chief Justice of South Wales was given to Lord Ferrers, an Englishman.

Rhys ap Gruffydd was popular with the people of South Wales and Henry VIII's decision created a great deal of bad feeling in the area. Lord Ferrers was accused of treating the Welsh people unfairly and in 1529 Rhys ap Gruffydd and forty armed men attempted to rescue a group of men imprisoned by Lord Ferrers in Carmarthen Castle.

---

(18) J. F. Rees, *Studies in Welsh History* (1947)
Sir Rhys ap Gruffydd... was charged with high treason... but, apart from the evidence of an informer... there appears to have been no basis for this accusation.

---

(19) Caroline Skeel, *Council in the Marches of Wales* (1904)
Elis Gruffydd says that when Sir Rhys ap Gruffydd went down to Wales the whole country turned out to welcome him, whereupon Lord Ferrers grew jealous. The two rivals happened to come to Carmarthen at the same time, and an open quarrel resulted from a fight between their supporters. They were promptly summoned before the Star Chamber... where they hurled at each other accusations of violence, oppression, and bribery. At last both parties were censured for their misdoings, Lord Ferrers especially for his bad temper and quarrelling with one young enough to be his son.

Henry VIII warned Rhys ap Gruffydd that he had to accept the authority of Lord Ferrers. A few months later a group of Rhys ap Gruffydd's men once again attacked Carmarthen Castle. This time Rhys ap Gruffydd was arrested and imprisoned in the Tower of London. When Rhys was brought to court he was charged with plotting Henry VIII's death and planning to make himself king of Wales. Although little evidence of this charge was produced in court, Rhys was found guilty and executed.

---

(20) David Williams, *A History of Modern Wales* (1977)
Rhys ap Gruffydd... was alleged to have conspired with others to obtain help from Ireland and Scotland to establish himself as ruler of Wales.

(21) G. E. Jones, *Modern Wales* (1984)
Rhys ap Gruffydd was executed in 1531. His was not the only Tudor execution to take place on the flimsiest of evidence. It seems likely that his real crime... was to be opposed to the annulment of Henry VIII's marriage with Catherine of Aragon.

(22) Elis Gruffydd, *Chronicle* (c. 1555)
It is unlikely that Sir Rhys was so foolish as to believe in his heart that the king of the Scots would in any way make him Prince of Wales if he succeeded in winning the crown.

3.1 Why was Rhys ap Gruffydd angry with Henry VIII and Lord Ferrers in 1525?

3.2 Look at the glossary on page 56 and then explain the meaning of high treason.

3.3 Was Rhys ap Gruffydd guilty of high treason? Select information from the sources to support your answer.

4. Law and Order

After Edward I conquered Wales in 1283, the country was separated into two distinct areas: the Principality and the Welsh Marches. The Principality was under the direct control of the king of England and was ruled on the same lines as English regions. The Principality was divided into shires (counties) which were governed by officials appointed by the king.

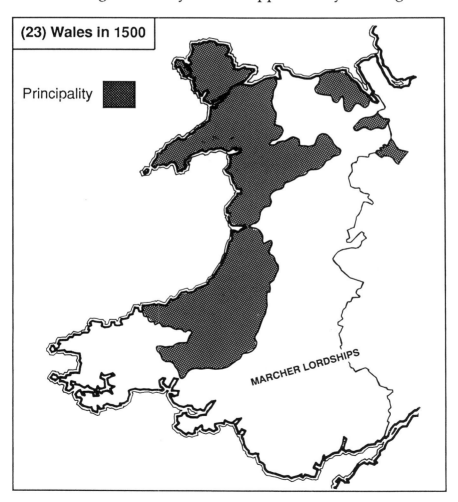

(23) Wales in 1500

Principality

MARCHER LORDSHIPS

The remaining two-thirds of Wales - the Welsh Marches - was ruled by Marcher Lords. These lords had their own laws and customs and had the power to arrange and collect taxes.

After Henry VIII became king he became increasingly concerned with the way that Marcher Lords ruled their lands. Reports he received suggested that some of the Marcher Lords were failing to maintain law and order. It was argued that criminals were breaking the law in England and then escaping to Wales. One report that Henry VIII received claimed that a corrupt official working in the lordship of Magor was receiving payment from twenty-three murderers and twenty-five thieves in return for protecting them from English justice.

In 1534, Parliament passed a series of laws that attempted to improve law and order in Wales. One law imposed restrictions on the carrying of weapons, another gave permission for English justices to enter Wales and arrest people wanted for crimes committed in England.

Henry VIII was also concerned about the old Welsh practice of arddel, a system under which, in return for money, a person in the locality could receive protection from a Marcher Lord. It was argued that the arddel system encouraged men to live under the protection of one lord while committing crimes in territory controlled by another. In 1534 Henry VIII's Parliament made the payment of arddel illegal.

---

(24) Sir Edward Croft, Vice-Chamberlain of the Council of the Marches, letter to Thomas Cromwell (7 March 1533)
Wales is out of order, and there have been many murders... no punishment has followed because the chiefs of the Council are spiritual men and cannot administer punishment of death... Some men should be sent down to use the sword of justice... Otherwise the Welsh will grow so wild it will not be easy to bring them into order again.

(25) Preamble of an Act of Parliament passed in 1535

There are many Lordship marches within the country of Wales in which the law cannot be used; where murders and house-burnings, robberies and riots are committed without fear of punishment and felons escape from justice by going from one lordship to another.

(26) Public executions (c. 1530)

Later that year Henry VIII appointed Rowland Lee, the bishop of Coventry, as President of the King's Council in the Marches of Wales. Lee was given instructions to restore law and order in the area. As well as punishing people who committed crimes in the Marches, Lee had the task of making sure that English criminals were taken back to their own shires for trial.

Lee imposed a reign of terror in Wales. Lee believed strongly that public executions helped deter others from committing crimes. Even the bodies of criminals killed while being arrested were taken to the nearest market town to be hung and displayed on the gallows.

(28) Rowland Lee, letter to Thomas Cromwell, King Henry VIII's chief minister (19 January 1536) Four outlaws were brought to us... Three were alive and one slain, brought in a sack. We have had him hanged on a gallows here for a sign... It was market day, and 300 people saw it... All thieves in Wales quake for fear.

(27) Thomas Cromwell, drawn by Hans Holbein in 1533.

(29) Rowland Lee, letter to Thomas Cromwell, (29 January, 1536)

I am informed that... Richard Lloyd of Welshpool stole cattle from... the baron of Burford... The baron ordered Lloyd's servants to be hanged... The hanging of Lloyd, a gentleman... would cause forty men to beware.

(30) Rowland Lee, letter to Thomas Cromwell (1538)

Wales was never in better order... Since Christmas I hear of neither stealing, riots, murders or manslaughters... In Wales... is order and quiet such as now in England.

(31) Ellis Gruffydd, *Chronicle* (c. 1555)
In 1534 there was much disorder... The King appointed Rowland Lee as President of his council in that part of Wales and gave him and his people full authority to administer punishment to those who merited it... It is said that over five thousand men were hanged within the space of six years.

(32) J. D. Mackie, *The Earlier Tudors* (1952)
Whether Rowland Lee really hanged 5,000 offenders may be doubted, but he certainly established the authority of the law, checking violence, fortifying castles and harbours, preventing large assemblies, and punishing jurors who refused to do their duty.

Rowland Lee thought it was particularly important to punish wealthy men who broke the law. When Lee arrested John Thomas of Kedewen for manslaughter, attempts were made to persuade Henry VIII to grant him a pardon. Lee wrote a letter to Henry VIII's chief minister claiming that to "hang such a gentleman in his county... would do more good than to hang a hundred poor men".

Rowland Lee's policy appeared to be effective and in 1538 he was able to report to Henry VIII that even in "the wildest parts of Wales" there was now "order and quiet".

4.1 What complaints did Henry VIII make about the way the Marcher Lords ruled their territory in Wales?

4.2 Describe the different methods that Henry VIII used to improve law and order in the Welsh Marches.

4.3 Compare the views of the authors of sources 31 and 32. What kind of documents would J. D. Mackie have needed to study before making these comments?

5. The Protestant Reformation in Wales

In 1517 Martin Luther, a monk from Wittenburg, Germany, began criticising the power and corruption of the Pope and the Catholic church. Luther attacked the Pope for pardoning people's sins in exchange for money. He thought it was immoral for the Pope's agents (pardoners) to travel all over Europe selling these letters of indulgence.

Luther also criticised the Pope for not allowing the Bible to be translated into other languages. Luther argued that as the vast majority of people could not read Latin, they had to rely on what the priest told them was the meaning of Biblical texts.

Henry VIII initially disagreed with Martin Luther. Henry feared that criticism of the Church might encourage people to criticise the monarchy. In 1521 he wrote a book attacking Luther's religious ideas. The Pope was so pleased with Henry's loyalty that he gave him the title 'Defender of the Faith'.

Henry's opinions about the views of the Pope changed after he was denied permission to divorce his first wife Catherine of Aragon. In 1534, Henry made himself head of the Church in England and Wales in place of the Pope. Although Henry continued to persecute Protestants, he became increasingly hostile to those who remained loyal to the Pope.

Only two members of the clergy in Wales refused to accept Henry as Head of the Church. The Bishop of Llandaff managed to escape to Spain, but Richard Fetherston, archdeacon of Brecon, was arrested after he refused to sign a declaration stating that Henry VIII's marriage to Catherine of Aragon was illegal. Fetherston, who was Catherine's personal chaplain, was imprisoned in the Tower of London for five and a half years. Despite this punishment Richard Fetherston still refused to accept Henry as Head of the Church, and in July, 1540 he was hung, drawn and quartered at Smithfield in London.

(33) The execution of William Tyndale (1563)

---

(34) William Tyndale, *Obedience of Christian Man* (1528)
All the prophets wrote in the mother tongue... Why then might they (the scriptures) not be written in the mother tongue? They will say, the scripture is so hard, that thou could never understand it... They will say it cannot be translated into our tongue... they are false liars.

One of the most important aspects of the Protestant religion was the belief that it was vitally important for people to be able to read the Bible for themselves. At first, Henry VIII was hostile to the idea. People caught distributing copies of Tyndale's English translation of the Bible were burnt at the stake.

In 1536 Henry changed his mind on the idea of an English translation and gave permission for the publication of the English Bible. He also ordered that a copy of the newly translated bible should be placed in every church in his kingdom. Henry still considered himself to be a Catholic, but by taking this action, he began to move the Church of England and Wales in the direction of Protestantism.

One of the most ardent supporters of Protestantism in Wales was John Price of Brecon. He pointed out that very few people in Wales understood the English language and were therefore unable to read the recently distributed bibles. Henry VIII was unimpressed with these arguments and refused to allow the Bible to be published in Welsh.

---

(35) William Salesbury, *Oll Synnwyr Pen Kembero Ygyd* (1546)
Go barefoot on pilgrimage to the King and his council to beg that the Holy Scriptures should be available in your language... If you do not wish utterly to depart from the faith of Christ... obtain the holy scripture in your own tongue.

(36) John Price, *Yny Lhyuyr Hwnn* (1547)
Since God has given the printing press... to multiply knowledge of His blessed words, it is proper for us, as all Christendom has done already, to participate in that virtue.

5.1 Explain why Henry VIII changed his views between the years 1520 and 1534 on the power of the Pope.

5.2 How did the Welsh clergy react to Henry VIII becoming Head of the Church in England and Wales?

5.3 Study sources 35 and 36 and then explain what William Salesbury and John Price wanted Henry VIII to do.

6. Union of England and Wales

Henry VIII's fears about the power of the Marcher Lords grew after his break with the Catholic church in 1534. Some of the Marcher lords remained loyal to the Pope and Henry was worried that they might rebel against him.

Henry was also warned that Catholic monarchs in France and Spain, who wanted to see the Pope's authority restored, might try to invade England by landing their soldiers on the poorly defended coasts of Wales. To secure his throne, Henry decided to take direct control of the whole of the kingdom, including the country of Wales.

In 1536 and 1543, the English Parliament passed legislation that later became known as the Act of Union. The Principality and the lands previously controlled by the Marcher Lords were now joined together to form a united Wales.

Under the Act of Union Wales was divided into thirteen shires. The administration of these shires was based on the English model with each shire having its own sheriff and justice of the peace.

The sheriff was responsible for the collection of local taxes. He also had the task of arresting law breakers and keeping them prisoner in the shire gaol until they could be dealt with by the local justice of the peace.

---

(37) On 12 March, 1536, Rowland Lee, President of the King's Council in the Marches of Wales wrote a letter to Thomas Cromwell, Henry VIII's chief minister.
I have been informed that the King wishes to make Wales... have justices of the peace as in England... I do not think it is sensible to have justices of the peace in Wales, for there are very few Welsh who have ten pounds of land, and their wisdom is less than their land.

(38) Henry VIII

(39) Act of Union: Introduction (1536)
His Majesty (Henry VIII) has as a singular love and favour
that he bears towards his subjects of Wales... He hath
ordained that Wales shall continue for ever... incorporated...
with his Realm of England... the people of Wales shall have
and enjoy all the freedoms, liberties, rights, privileges and
laws... as the king's subjects born with the realm have.

(40) In 1536 Eustace Chapuys sent a letter to King Charles I of Spain.
The distress of the people is incredible, especially the Welsh, from whom by act of parliament the king has just taken away their native laws, customs and privileges.

(41) William Salesbury, *Dictionary in English and Welsh* (1547)
King Henry showed excellent wisdom when he decided that there shall be no difference in laws and language between his subjects in... Wales and his subjects in England.

(42) Sir John Davies, *A Discovery of the True Causes Why Ireland Was Never Entirely Subdued* (1612)
Henry VIII... united the dominion of Wales to England and divided it into shires... and made all the laws and statues of England in force there.... in a short period Wales was securely settled in peace and obedience.

(43) John Bowle, *Henry VIII* (1964)
In 1536 Henry had created new shires and boroughs, all now represented in the English Parliament. English law had superseded tribal custom... those unable to speak English were excluded from office... Most of the people accepted these measures since they were intensely loyal to the Tudor dynasty and felt that Henry had their interests at heart.

(44) Gwyn Jones, *The Tudor Period in Wales* (1921)
The Tudor policy of pretending that Welshmen were Englishmen may have been kindly meant, and it may have been better than any other way of repression, but to become sentimental over the supposition that it converted a land of wild anarchy into a perfect paradise... is a matter for laughter.

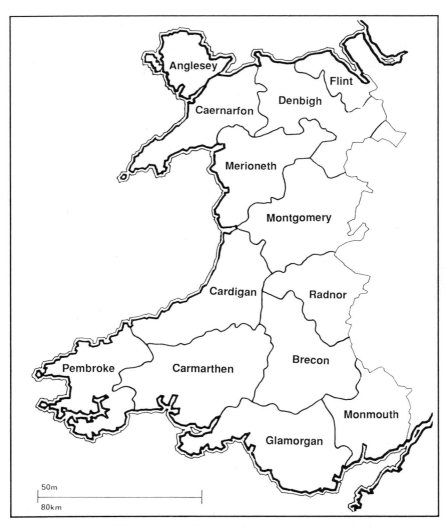

Anglesey
Flint
Denbigh
Caernarfon
Merioneth
Montgomery
Cardigan
Radnor
Brecon
Pembroke
Carmarthen
Monmouth
Glamorgan

50m
80km

(45) Wales after the Act of Union

(46) E. Roland Williams, *Elizabethan Wales* (1924)
The Act of 1535... need not be interpreted as being evidence
of any contempt or hatred for the Welsh... it was mainly as a
matter of administrative convenience... it was obviously
simpler to have one official language... instead of two.

(47) Prys Morgan and David Thomas, *Wales, The Shaping of a Nation* (1985)
The effects of the Acts of Union... are now frequently seen as the beginning of the end of Wales and the Welsh. They undermined the dominance of the Welsh language by proscribing it for many official and almost all legal purposes... they encouraged the decline of Welsh cultural life, replacing it with a London-based culture.

(48) William Owen Williams, *The Survival of the Welsh Language After the Union* (1964)
In Wales the small, scattered rural communities were self-contained and closely-knit... To these people a journey to a neighbouring parish was an event; to the nearest market town, an adventure... In such communities as these, it is no wonder that the Welsh language survived.

Some English people objected to the idea of Wales being administered by the Welsh people. Roland Lee, President of the King's Council in the Marches of Wales, argued that the Welsh would be incapable of enforcing law and order in Wales.

For the first time in history, an attempt was made to define the territorial boundaries of Wales. In some cases, land was lost to England. The Welsh-speaking town of Oswestry now became part of the English county of Shropshire. Herefordshire and Gloucestershire also received land that had previously been controlled by Marcher Lords in Wales.

Under the terms of the Act of Union, Wales was granted permission to be represented in Parliament. In 1542, twenty-seven people in Wales were elected to sit in the House of Commons as members of parliament. Most of these elections were not contested and the person sent to Parliament was usually selected by a few wealthy families in the area.

(49) Raymond Grant, *The Parliamentary History of Glamorgan* (1978)
Landowners gave their tenants their instructions as how they were to vote... Tenants who voted contrary to their landlord's wishes were liable to be turned out of their farms.

(50) Members of Parliament for Glamorgan, 1542-1604. All these men were elected unopposed. The first time there was a contested election was in 1734.

1542	George Herbert	grandson of the 1st Earl of Pembroke
1547	John Bassett	large landowner from Llantrithyd
1553	George Matthew	son of a man knighted at Bosworth.
1553	Anthony Mansel	son of Rice Mansel, owner of Margam estates, and John Bassett's son-in-law
1554	Edward Mansel	son of Rice Mansel
1554	Edward Carne	worked as lawyer for Henry VIII
1558	William Herbert	son of George Herbert elected in1542
1559	William Herbert	grandson of George Herbert elected in 1542
1563	William Bassett	son-in-law of Sir Rice Mansel
1584	Robert Sydney	2nd Earl of Pembroke's brother-in-law
1586	Thomas Carne	son of Edward Carne elected in 1554
1597	Thomas Mansel	son of Edward Mansel elected in1554
1601	John Herbert	son of William Herbert elected in 1559
1604	Philip Herbert	son of Henry, 2nd Earl of Pembroke

(51) G. Dyfnallt Owen, Elizabethan Wales (1964)
In 1601, Sir John Salesbury, squire of Llewenni, decided to make a bid for the county seat of Denbighshire. His opponent was Sir Richard Trevor... Both parties made no pretence of allowing the freeholders of the shire to judge their respective merits as candidates. They simply terrorised those who were within reach of their strong arm.

One aspect of the Act of Union in particular upset a large number of people in Wales. Clause 17 declared that all people who were chosen to represent Wales as officials or Members of Parliament were required to speak English.

After the Act of Union, the king's courts replaced the manor courts in Wales. The Act of Union stipulated that all court proceedings should be in the "English tongue". At this time only a very small percentage of the population in Wales could speak English. Although latimers (translators) were allowed in court, many Welsh men and women believed that this new ruling prevented them from obtaining true justice.

The Act of Union also made changes to land inheritance in Wales. In 1543 Gravelkind, the system by which a man's sons inherited his land in equal shares was abolished, and replaced by the English system of sole inheritance by the eldest son.

---

(52) George Owen, *Description of Pembrokeshire* (1603)
'Gravelkind' was used among Welshmen... in the process of time the whole country was brought into small pieces of ground and intermingled up and down one with another, so as in every five or six acres you shall have ten or twelve owners.

6.1   Give as many reasons as you can for Henry VIII's decision to form a united Wales in 1536.

6.2   Why were some people in Wales opposed to the Act of Union?

6.3   What was Gravelkind? Why was it abolished in 1543?

6.4   Study sources 49 and 50 and read about the Herbert and Mansel families on pages 59-62. (i) Explain the influence that these two families had on the selection of the members of parliament for Glamorgan. (ii) Why were there no contested parliamentary elections between 1542 and 1734?

7. Dissolution of the Monasteries

At the beginning of the 16th century, monasteries owned well over a quarter of all the cultivated land in England and Wales. In England farmers who rented land from the monks often criticised them for being greedy and uncaring landlords. It was also claimed that the monks had been corrupted by the wealth accumulated through land ownership.

The situation in Wales was slightly different. Monasteries in Wales tended to be smaller and poorer than those in England. Most of the Welsh monasteries only housed five or six monks. In 1535 the total income of the forty-six religious houses in Wales only amounted to £3,178. This was less than the income of just one of the larger monasteries in England.

In August 1535, King Henry VIII sent a team of officials to investigate the monasteries in England and Wales. Henry's officials found that some of the monks and nuns were doing good work in teaching and helping the poor living in their area. However, they also discovered that in many monasteries the monks were spending their wealth on themselves.

---

(53) Lord Ferrers, letter to Thomas Cromwell (1532)
We have found a monk at Strata Florida making false coins in his chamber in the abbey and now have him in Carmarthen jail.

(54) Geoffrey Baskerville, *The Suppression of the Monasteries* (1937)
Abbot Salisbury of Valle Crucis seems to have been a forerunner of motor bandits, and in May 1535 was caught robbing an Oxfordshire gentleman on the highway. He was an expert forger and spent long years in the Tower of London after he was detected.

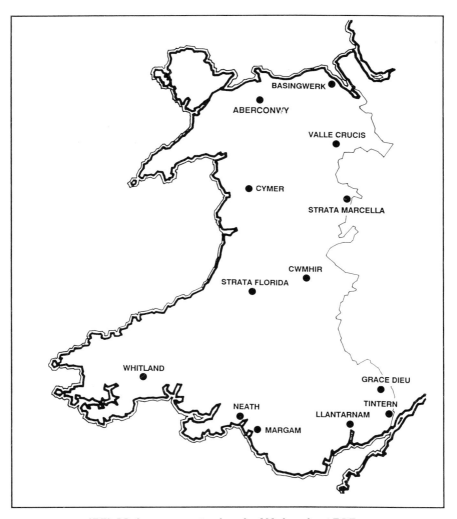

(55) Main monasteries in Wales in 1535

(56) John Vaughan of Carmarthen, letter to Thomas Cromwell (November, 1535)
The Bishop of Llandaff and his archdeacon are not only guilty of allowing the ruin and decay of their mansion but of other great faults.

31

In a few cases monks were even found to be involved in criminal activities. It was claimed that the monks at Strata Florida were making forged coins while the abbot of Valle Crucis Abbey was accused of being involved in highway robbery. Reports from other monasteries in Wales suggested that although monks took vows of celibacy some of them, including the abbots of Margam and Conwy, had wives and children.

After reading these reports Henry VIII decided to close down all the smaller monasteries. Of the 376 monasteries that were closed, 24 were in Wales. This included the monastery at Carmarthen, which had been highly praised in the report for its charity and hospitality.

---

(57) David Robinson, *Tintern Abbey* (1986)
Tintern Abbey was surrendered to the king's visitors on 3 September 1536... The abbey silver, plate and ornaments were catalogued, weighed and sent to the king's treasury... The lead was quickly stripped from the roofs and its profits reserved for the king... Eventually, in 1546 part, if not all, of this was bought for £166 by the earl of Worcester, probably for building work at his castles at Chepstow and Raglan.

(58) Glanmor Williams, *The Dissolution of the Monasteries* (1967)
As far as is known... the closing of the monasteries in Glamorgan ... caused no upheaval or serious protest. There is no surviving record that a voice was raised or a hand lifted, on behalf of these once influential houses... The only individuals who could benefit were those who had ready cash or who could raise it quickly. Quite often they were men who had done well out of service to the Crown... To acquire their new estates they were often able to raise impressive sums; Rice Mansel, for instance, put up no less than £2,600 in all for the estates of Margam Abbey.

Hæc dicit dominus de⁹.

Sic dicit Papa,

(59) 'The word of God, against the word of the Pope' (c. 1538)

Henry VIII sent Richard Ingworth, the bishop of Dover, to close down the monasteries in Wales. Bishop Ingworth and his men arrived in Wales in August, 1538. Valuable objects owned by the monasteries were sent to the royal treasury in London. Other property such as musical instruments, glass windows and wooden furniture were auctioned off to local people.

The land owned by the monasteries was taken over by Bishop Ingworth and then sold off cheaply to nobles and merchants. They in turn sold some of the lands to smaller farmers. This process meant that a large number of people had good reason to support Henry VIII's actions.

The Religious Shrine of Derfel Gadarn

(60) Ellis Price, letter to Thomas Cromwell, (6 April, 1538)
There is an image of Derfel Gadarn... in whom the people have so great confidence, hope and trust, that they come daily unto him... some with oxen or horses, and the rest with money...There is a common saying that whoever will offer anything to the image of Derfel Gadarn... will get out of hell when they are damned.

(61) Friar Forest was burnt at the stake for opposing Henry VIII's divorce from Catherine of Aragon. The wooden carving of Derfel Gadarn was burnt at the same time. This poem was attached to the scaffold.
David Derfel Gadarn,
As sayeth the Welshmen,
Fetched outlaws out of Hell.
Now he is come, with spear and shield,
In harness to burn in Smithfield,
For in Wales he may not dwell.
And Forest the friar,
The obstinate liar,
That wilfully shall be dead,
In the contumacy
The Gospel doth deny,
And the King to be Supreme Head.

(62) Edward Hall, *Chronicle* (1538)
A little before the execution of Friar Forest, a huge and great image was brought to the gallows... the image was brought out of Wales... an image much sought and worshipped by Welshmen. The image was called Derfel Gadarn... The Welshmen had a prophecy that this image should set a whole forest a fire, which prophecy now took effect, for he set this Friar Forest on fire and consumed him to nothing.

The monasteries at Carmarthen, Brecon, Bangor and Strata Marcella were turned into schools. The remaining monasteries were demolished to ensure that the monks did not return after the king's officials had left the area. The lead sheets used to cover monastery roofs were stripped off and melted down. Some of the lead was sold to local merchants, the rest was transported back to London.

In 1538, Henry turned his attention to religious shrines. For hundreds of years pilgrims had visited shrines that contained important religious relics. Wealthy pilgrims often gave very expensive jewels and ornaments to the monks that looked after these holy places. Henry decided that the shrines should be closed down and any wealth that had been accumulated given to the crown.

The most important shrine in Wales was at Llandderfel. Henry VIII's officials reported that as many as 600 people a day came to see the image of the local saint, Derfel Gadarn. Henry ordered that the large wooden sculpture of Derfel be taken to Smithfield and burnt at the stake. Other religious shrines in Wales such as those at Winifred's Well, Penrhys and Bangor were also destroyed.

---

(63) Roger Lockyer, *Tudor and Stuart Britain* (1985)
The decision to dissolve the monasteries was taken primarily for financial, not moral reasons. Henry VIII's wars had left him desperately short of money... He was casting around for new sources of revenue, and the monasteries were an obvious target.

(64) David Robinson, *Tintern Abbey* (1986)
The Dissolution of the Monasteries was part of the king's policy to establish total control over the Church in his realm. But in addition to severing links with Rome, their suppression was a source of considerable wealth to the Crown.

The Pope and members of the Catholic Church were very upset when they heard the news that Henry was destroying religious shrines. On 17 December 1538, the Pope announced to the Christian world that Henry had been excommunicated from the Catholic church.

Henry now had nothing to lose and he closed down the rest of the monasteries and nunneries in England and Wales. This included those at Strata Florida, Whitland and Neath. All told, Henry closed down over 850 monastic houses between 1536 and 1540. Monks and nuns who did not oppose Henry's policies were granted pensions. However, these regular payments of money did not allow for the rapid inflation that was taking place at that time and within a few years most monks and nuns were in a state of extreme poverty.

7.1   How did monasteries in Wales differ from those in England?

7.2   What criticisms did Henry VIII's officials make of English and Welsh monks?

7.3   Study sources 60, 61 and 62. (i) Why did people from Wales visit the image of Derfel Gadarn at Llandderfel? (ii) Why did Henry VIII arrange for the image to be destroyed?

7.4   Write an extended account of why Henry VIII closed down the monasteries in England and Wales. In your account give the different reasons for closing down the monasteries and make a judgement on the relative importance of each reason.

8. Protestants and Catholics

When Henry VIII died in 1547, his only son Edward was nine years old. Edward was too young to rule, so his uncle, the Duke of Somerset took over the running of the country.

The Duke of Somerset was a Protestant who held strong opinions on religion. Attempts were now made to destroy those aspects of religion that were associated with the Catholic church. Features in churches that offended Protestants were destroyed. Stained glass windows were removed and wall paintings were covered by whitewash.

In 1549 the Latin service was abolished and replaced by one that was based on the recently published English Book of Common Prayer. To the majority of people in Wales this new service was no more intelligible than those services previously conducted in Latin. The situation improved when, in 1551, William Salesbury published his 'Kynniver Llith a Ban', a Welsh translation of the epistles and gospels of the Prayer Book.

The most prominent Protestant in Wales was Robert Ferrar, the Bishop of St Davids. When, in 1549, priests were also given the legal right to take wives, Ferrar was one of the first members of the clergy to get married. The following year he ordered that altars in the churches in his diocese should be taken away and replaced by communion tables.

---

(66) John Davies, *A History of Wales* (1990)
Because of Mary's determination to re-establish the Roman Catholic religion, almost five hundred of her subjects fled to mainland Europe... There were about a dozen Welshmen among the exiles... The majority of the Welsh people probably supported Mary's efforts. That, at least, is what is suggested by the work of the poets; to them Protestantism was 'the English religion'.

(67) Queen Mary by Master John (1544)

The Duke of Somerset had made sure that Edward VI was educated as a Protestant, hoping that when Edward was old enough to rule he would continue the policy of supporting the

Protestant religion. However, when Edward VI was fifteen he died of tuberculosis.

The next in line to the throne was King Henry VIII's eldest daughter, Mary. As her mother was Catherine of Aragon, Mary had been brought up as a devout Catholic. To protect herself against the Protestants, Mary decided to try to form an alliance with the Catholic monarchies in Europe. In 1554, Mary married Philip, the eldest son of King Charles of Spain.

Soon after her marriage, Mary declared that the Pope was the only true head of the Church. This was followed by the execution of Thomas Cranmer, the Archbishop of Canterbury and other Protestants who refused to accept the religious authority of the Pope.

Except for a few areas such as Carmarthen and Cardiff, people in Wales had been unenthusiastic about the Protestant reforms and were willing to accept a return to Catholicism. However, there were those who refused to change. Some Welsh clergy fled abroad but others stayed and were punished. Robert Ferrar, Bishop of St Davids in Wales, was burnt at the stake at Carmarthen in 1555. Two other Protestants in Wales, William Nichol from Haverfordwest and Rawlins White from Cardiff, were also executed for their religious beliefs.

---

(68) *Grey Friars Chronicle* (1548)
On St Martin's Day Bishop Ferrar... preached at St Paul's... against all manner of things of the Church and the Sacrament of the Altar, vestments, copes, altars, and all other things.

(69) John Foxe, *Book of Martyrs* (1563)
Robert Ferrar... refused to recant his heresies, schisms, and errors... Thus this godly bishop... was brought to the place of execution in Carmarthen... on the the 30th March... sustained the torments of the fire.

(70) John Dane witnessed the execution of Rawlins White in Cardiff in 1555.

Rawlins White, a fisherman from Cardiff... was brought from Cockmarell Prison... The smith came with a great chain of iron... As he cast the chain about him... Rawlins said, "I pray you friend, knock in the chain fast" When the smith had made him sure, the officers began to lay on more wood with a little straw and reed... Then someone cried out, "Set to fire"... the straw and reed cast up a great and sudden flame; in which this blessed man bathed his hands until the fat dropped away... All this while he cried with a loud voice, "O lord, receive my soul," until he could not open his mouth... Thus died this godly man for the testimony of God's truth, being now rewarded no doubt with the crown of everlasting life.

8.1　What religious changes took place during the reign of:
　　　(i) Edward VI; (ii) Mary I?

8.2　Study source 66. What evidence does the author provide to sustain his view that the "majority of the Welsh people probably supported Mary's efforts"? What other information could the author have used to support his point of view?

8.3　Describe the views of Robert Ferrar.

8.4　Write a short essay on religious martyrs in Tudor Wales. You will need to read pages 20-22, 37-42 and 58-59 before answering the question. In your essay you should include a discussion on the following: (i) why monarchs ordered the execution of people for their religious beliefs; (ii) why people like Robert Ferrar, Rawlins White and William Davies were willing to die for their religious beliefs.

9. The Welsh Bible

In 1558, Queen Mary began to get pains in her stomach and
thought she was pregnant. This was important to Mary as she
wanted to ensure that a Catholic monarchy would continue
after her death. It was not to be. Mary had stomach cancer.
When Mary died later that year, Henry VIII's other daughter,
Elizabeth, a Protestant, became queen of England.

(71) Painting of Queen Elizabeth in 1559

(72) Pledge signed by Anthony Kitchen, Bishop of Llandaff on 12 July, 1559
I accept and obey the whole course of religion now approved in the state of her Grace's Realm.

(73) William Haugaard, *Elizabeth and the English Reformation* (1968)
Of the sixteen bishops Queen Elizabeth placed in the four sees (in Wales), twelve were natives and one a Welsh-speaking Englishman - a proportion which has seldom been greater, before or since.

With the help of her chief minister, William Cecil, Elizabeth set about making Britain a Protestant nation again. Catholic bishops appointed by Mary were replaced by Protestants. In 1559, Parliament passed the Act of Uniformity which meant that now everybody in England and Wales had to attend Protestant church services.

The majority of the clergy in Wales accepted the return to the Protestant religion without complaint. A few attempted to stay true to the old faith of Catholicism. One group lived and worshipped in a cave at Little Orme in Caernarfonshire. Led by Father William Davies, the group began printing Welsh translations of Catholic books. These were probably the first books ever to be printed in Wales. The authorities found out about the activities of Davies and the cave was raided. Davies escaped but he was eventually arrested while trying to leave the country at Holyhead. Soon afterwards Davies was hung, drawn and quartered at Beaumaris Castle.

The main priority of Protestant leaders in Wales was to obtain Welsh translations of religious books. In 1563, a group of Welshmen led by William Salesbury obtained permission from Parliament to produce a Welsh Bible and a Welsh Prayer Book.

William Salesbury and Richard Davies, Bishop of St Asaph, were the two main people involved in the translations of these religious books. As Welsh was not a standardised language the translation was a complicated process. A Welsh version of the Book of Common Prayer and the New Testament appeared in 1567. Some Welsh people were unhappy with the translation, claiming that Davies and Salesbury had over-emphasised the Latin elements of the language.

Davies and Salesbury had originally planned to translate the Old Testament as well, but hurt by criticism of their version of the New Testament, decided to abandon the project.

(74) British stamp published in 1988.

(75) William Salesbury, *Oll Synnwyr Pen Kembero Ygyd* (1547)
If you do not wish to be worse than animals... obtain learning in your own language; if you do not wish to be more unnatural than any other nation under the sun, love your language... And take this advice from me: unless you save and correct and perfect the language before the extinction of the present generation, it will be too late afterwards... If you do not wish utterly to depart from the faith of Christ... obtain the holy scripture in your own tongue.

(76) Letter sent by the Bishop of Bangor to Sir William Cecil, Queen Elizabeth's chief minister, on 7th October, 1567.
I find by my small experience among them here that ignorance continues... Since I came to Wales I have found images and altars standing in churches, much pilgrimage going on, many candles set up to honour the saints and relics carried about... Chiefly because of the clergy (there are not six who can preach in Welsh in these three shires) ... God's word is in an unknown tongue.

(77) William Morgan, dedication written on the Welsh Bible presented to Queen Elizabeth (1588)
Similarity and agreement in religion rather than in speech much more promotes unity.

(78) Morris Kyffin, *Deffynniad Ffydd Eglwys Loegr* (1594)
A Churchman from Wales declared... that the printing of Welsh books should not be allowed, for the Welsh should be made to learn English and to forget the Welsh... Could the Devil himself have expressed it better?

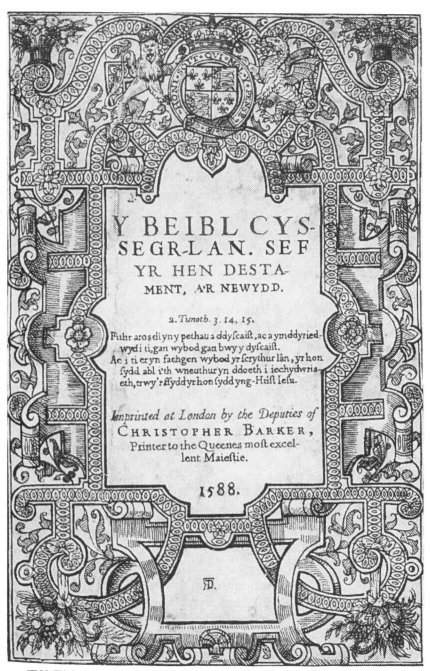

(79) Title page of William Morgan's Welsh Bible (1588)

In 1582, William Morgan, vicar of Llanrhaeadr-ym-Mochnant, began work on the mammoth task of translating the whole Bible into Welsh. As well as providing the first translation of the Old Testament, Morgan also made changes to Salesbury's version of the New Testament.

A number of people living in Llanrhaeadr-ym-Mochnant complained that Morgan was spending too much time on the translation of the Bible and not enough time looking after their needs. Some of Morgan's parishioners even wrote a letter of complaint to the Archbishop of Canterbury. However, the leaders of the Church wanted a Welsh version of the Bible and Morgan was encouraged to continue with the project.

Morgan's Welsh Bible was published in 1588. Within a few months there was a Welsh Bible in every parish church in Wales. As a result of Morgan's work religious services could now be held in Welsh; this helped to undermine the view that the Protestant religion was an English religion imposed on the Welsh people.

---

(80) John Davies, *A History of Wales* (1990)
In 1563, the bishops of Wales... were commanded to ensure that a Welsh version of the Bible and the Prayer Book would be available in every parish church in Wales... The intention that the Welsh should learn English was not abandoned; the act of 1563 insisted that in the churches of Wales the English Bible should be available alongside the Welsh Bible in the hope that the Welsh in dealing with both languages together, would rapidly master English.

(81) John Roland Phillips, *The Civil War in Wales* (1874)
An Act was passed by Elizabeth, in 1563, authorising the translation of the Bible into Welsh. This Act ordained that a copy of the work when printed should be placed in every parish church and chapel in Wales.

(82) William Williams, _The Survival of the Welsh Language After the Union_ (1964)
Scriptural authority was the very foundation of Protestantism and it is no wonder that the Welsh reformers should have been so determined that, since the Welsh people could not be expected to read the Bible in English, they should therefore be enabled to read it in their own language.

(83) Gruffyd Robert, letter to the Earl of Pembroke (1567)
My lord, the heart of every Welshman leaps with true joy when he hears a man of your eminence speaking his language.

(84) Sir John Wynn, commenting on his son marrying Bridget Grey from England, (December, 1606)
A gentle good soul, sensible and willing to please... should soon acquire the Welsh tongue.

9.1   Why did William Davies dislike the Act of Uniformity?

9.2   Why did Queen Elizabeth demand that bishops signed pledges like the one in source 72?

9.3   Give two reasons why it was decided to publish source 74 in 1988.

9.4   Study sources 75, 76, 78, 83 and 84. Do you think these writers were for or against the production of a Welsh Bible?

9.5   Until 1563 British monarchs had always insisted that there should not be a Welsh version of the Bible. Give as many reasons as you can why Queen Elizabeth gave permission for the production of a Welsh Bible. It will help you to read sources 76, 77, 80 and 82 before answering this question.

10. Elizabethan Wales

Queen Elizabeth I became queen of England and Wales in 1558. During her forty-five year reign, the population of Wales grew rapidly. The increased demand for food combined with a series of bad harvests in the 1580s, resulted in higher food prices.

Farming now became more profitable and this encouraged prosperous landlords to buy up land from the smaller farmers. Landlords also increased the rents of the remaining tenant farmers to ensure that the land would eventually return to them. In many areas of Wales rents doubled every few years. It was not long before some tenant farmers could not afford to pay these rents and were forced to leave the land.

(85) Price Index of different arable crops, 1570-1600

	wheat	barley	oats	rye	peas	beans
1570	265	296	291	345	239	220
1580	379	537	405	456	304	310
1590	394	720	757	652	592	541
1600	485	816	962	808	548	537

(86) In 1569 John Price complained to the Star Chamber about local reaction to his attempts to enclose common land in Neath.
A band of men destroyed the hedges... and then, with great and loud voices they said that they would continue as long as one hedge or mound was still standing.

(87) Woodcutting (c. 1520)

(88) Baptisms in Wales, 1570-1630

1570	323,665
1600	343,879
1630	387,177

(89) **Proceedings of the Star Chamber (1573)**
Sir Rowland Hayward of London, accuses Griffith ap Hugh... of leading fifty people at five o'clock in the morning, to cast down enclosures at Dolycoed.

(90) **G. Dyfnallt Owen, *Elizabethan Wales* (1964)**
When Gruffydd Nanney, a squire of the estate of that name in Merioneth, enclosed a portion of common woodland near Dolgellau with a stone wall, it was immediately thrown down and he was warned of more unpleasant consequences if he dared to rebuild it.

In some areas farmers lost their rights to graze their animals on common land. This land was now enclosed and used exclusively by the local landowner. One Welsh writer claimed that, by 1578, the whole of the Vale of Glamorgan had been enclosed. The Earl of Worcester, who owned large estates in South Wales, was particularly active in enclosing land. In 1590, the earl announced that he intended to take back over 3,000 acres, which he claimed farmers had been using illegally.

The enclosure of the common land posed a serious threat to small farmers. The commons were not only used to graze animals, but also provided them with rabbits for food, and wood which could be used for building or fuel for cooking and heating.

In many areas the small farmers attempted to resist the enclosure of the common land. Stone walls and hedges were destroyed and threats of violence were sent to the landlords who were planning to enclose the commons. In some instances the farmers were successful, but in most cases, the prospects of high profits encouraged landowners to use all the means available to enclose their land.

Unable to make a living from farming some Welshmen joined the army. Of the 100,000 men who served in the Tudor army between 1585 and 1600, about 9,000 came from Wales.

(91) A petition signed by farmers in Radnorshire and Montgomeryshire and sent to the Council of Wales in November, 1573.
Living near to mountains... we have few acres of land... some of it is barren... there is not enough pasture for the animals... without commons... we cannot maintain ourselves.

(92) Proceedings of the Star Chamber (1588)
John Vaughan, accuses Rees ap Richard and Thomas ap Richard of leading an armed assembly of 200 persons in an attempt to stop the enclosing of common land in Ffynant. The defendants are also accused of assaulting John Vaughan's servants while they were digging ditches.

(93) A Tudor coal mine (c. 1550)

Some farmers found alternative employment in mining. For hundreds of years, people in Wales had mined coal by digging small and shallow 'bell-pits'. This coal was normally for local use. However, the increasing demand for coal encouraged the sinking of deeper mines. Coal mines were opened in Swansea, Neath and Llanelli with shafts sunk to a depth of a 100 feet. In

Flintshire the coal mines were so deep that miners experienced problems with fire-damp. Some of the coal that was mined from pits close to rivers and coastal waters was exported to England, Ireland and France.

The gradual destruction of English forests (which had provided fuel for the furnaces of Kent and Sussex) had resulted in a search for new places to site ironworks. Ironmasters were attracted to Monmouthshire and Glamorgan where there were large supplies of both iron ore and wood-based fuel.

Richard Hanbury arrived from London in 1565 and soon established a successful ironworks at Blaenavon. Within a few years Hanbury was employing 200 local men as miners, woodcutters and charcoal makers. However, some people living in the area began to worry about the destruction of the local forests. After three years of iron production, over 6,000 beech trees had been cut down by Hanbury's men.

---

(94) George Owen, *Description of Pembrokeshire* (1603)
Miners sink their pits about four feet wide... they draw up the coals in a barrel.. by a rope.

(95) Celia Fiennes toured Wales in 1688. In her journal she described a visit to Flintshire.
The place is called Flintshire... It is a hilly place with many very high hills... There are quarries of stone, copper and iron mines... There are great coal pits... They have great wheels that are turned with horses that draw up the water and so drain the mines... they also have engines that draw up the coal in baskets... the people speak Welsh... the people go barefoot and bare-legged.

Sports and Pastimes

(96) A. H. Dodd, *The Social Order in Wales* (1952)
Knappan... a sort of primitive and more bloodthirsty rugby, played with a wooden ball by whole villages (on horseback and afoot) on occasional Sundays and certain fixed holy-days... Knappan was... more characteristic of south-west Wales... Other brands of football were popular farther north.

(97) George Owen, *Description of Pembrokeshire* (1603)
The ball is called knappan... and is made of wood... it should be boiled in tallow, to make it slippery, and hard to hold... One of the company hurl it in the air... He that catch it hurl it towards the place he playeth for... the knappan is tossed backward and forward, by throws... in three or four throws.. the knappan can move half a mile or more...The play is not over until the knappan be so far... that there is no hope to return it back that night... You see players return home with broken heads, black faces, bruised bodies, and lame legs.

(98) G. Dyfnallt Owen, *Elizabethan Wales* (1964)
It was not unknown for some players to equip themselves with pikestaffs and other weapons... Llangatwg and Crickhowell were noted rivals in Brecknock, and it was during the course of one game of football in 1579 that a Crickhowell player was thrown so heavily to the ground that he died... A fatal collision at Tregaron, in Cardiganshire between two contending footballers... frightened the survivor to such an extent that he chose to flee the country.

(99) Humphrey Llwyd, *Breviary of Britain* (1573)
The men of Montgomeryshire are addicted to idleness and unprofitable games. Whereby it come to pass that you shall find many rich English farmers amongst them whereas the landlords themselves... become very poor.

Queen Elizabeth, as with previous monarchs, insisted upon the exclusive rights to the metal ores needed to produce coins. In 1568, Queen Elizabeth granted the company Mines Royal monopoly rights to work lead and copper mines in England and Wales.

The main lead-mines in Wales were in Cardiganshire. By 1592 the district produced 30% of the lead smelted in Britain. Most of this lead was exported overseas. One lead-mine run by Thomas Myddelton was said to make a profit of over £2,000 a month.

In 1584, the Mines Royal company began transporting copper ore from their Cornwall mines to be smelted in Neath. Attracted by the region's large supplies of coal and timber, the company invested heavily in the Aberdulais plant, which was soon capable of processing 560 tons of copper ore a week.

10.1   How does source 88 help to explain the information in source 85?

10.2   What was enclosure? Why was there an increase in enclosure in Wales in the second-half of the 16th century?

10.3   Study sources 86, 89, 90, 91 and 92. What methods did Welsh farmers use to try to stop enclosure?

10.4   How did knappan differ from the modern game of rugby?

10.5   Write an essay on why the mining industry grew in Wales in the second-half of the 16th century. In your essay you should include a discussion on the following: (i) enclosure; (ii) the destruction of English forests; (iii) natural resources; (iv) transport; (v) Mines Royal; (vi) profitability.

GLOSSARY

ANGLICAN CHURCH The Church of England and Wales established during the Protestant Reformation.

ARABLE Land on which corn and other crops are grown.

ARCHDEACON A clergyman who is the bishop's main assistant.

ARDDEL System under which, in return for money, a person could receive protection from a Marcher Lord. Arddel was made illegal in 1534.

BAILIFF An official employed by a sheriff to serve writs and to make arrests.

BARD A poet-singer who composed, sang, or recited verses on heroes and their deeds.

BRAGOT A popular drink in Tudor Wales. Bragot was made by heating a mixture of beer, sugar and spices.

CHAMBERLAIN Chief officer of a royal or noble household.

CHANCELLOR The head of the Chancery. The Chancellor supervised the issue of royal charters, writs and letters.

CHARTERS Legal documents issued by a ruler or government. Charters mainly dealt with the ownership of land and the granting of privileges to towns.

COMMON LAND Land belonging to, or shared by, the community.

CONSTABLE A warden or governor of a castle or fortified town.

CORONER A member of the royal household charged with protecting the private property of the monarch.

DIOCESE An area under the control of a bishop.

ENCLOSURE An area of land formed as a result of enclosing with fences, ditches or hedges. In the 16th century people became very angry when the common land was enclosed and covered with grazing sheep.

EXCOMMUNICATION Expulsion from the Catholic Church. It was believed that all people who had contact with those who had been excommunicated would also suffer. Excommunicated people were therefore treated like lepers.

FELON A person who has committed a serious crime.

FIRE-DAMP A highly inflammable gas, consisting chiefly of methane, found underground in mines.

GRAVELKIND A system where a man's sons inherited his land in equal shares. It was the traditional inheritance system in Wales before it was made illegal by a law passed by parliament in 1543.

HERESY Religious beliefs that were in opposition to those held by the leaders of the Christian church. If heretics could not be persuaded to accept the traditional views of the Church they were likely to be executed.

HIGH TREASON A crime that involved any attempt to kill or remove a king or queen from power. Even people who criticised the monarchy were in danger of being charged with High Treason. The punishment for this crime was to be hanged, drawn and quartered. The condemned man was dragged through the streets by a horse and then hanged until nearly dead. After being revived, the prisoner had his heart cut out. The body was cut into four and displayed in different towns as a warning to others.

INDULGENCE A paper issued by the Roman Catholic Church that forgave people for sins they had committed. The selling of indulgences enabled the church to raise a great deal of money.

INFLATION A substantial rise in the general level of prices.

JUSTICIAR Chief officer under the king. The justiciar usually took over the running of the government when the king was out of the country.

PAPACY The system of government of the Roman Catholic Church of which the Pope is the supreme leader.

PARISH An area under the jurisdiction of a priest.

PARDONER Travelling priest who sold letters from the pope forgiving people for their sins.

PRINCIPALITY An area of Wales under the direct control of the English monarch. The Principality and the Welsh Marches were joined together to form a united Wales in 1536.

PROTESTANTS Name given to to those Christians that broke away from the Roman Catholic Church during the Reformation.

REFORMATION A religious movement that wanted reform of the doctrines and practices of the Roman Catholic Church.

RELIC An object that was claimed by the church to be connected in some way to Jesus Christ or one of the saints.

SHERIFF The king's representative in a shire or county.

SHRINES Holy places that kept religious relics. Henry VIII closed shrines in England and Wales in 1538.

USHER A doorkeeper employed by royal and noble households.

UPLAND An area of high land.

YEOMAN A farmer who possessed land with an annual value of over 40 shillings. Yeomen could serve on juries and vote in elections.

Welsh Tudor Biographies

Richard Davies was born in Conwy in 1501. After finishing his education at Oxford University Davies became vicar of Burnham Church in Buckinghamshire. A strong supporter of Protestant reforms, Davies was one of the first vicars in Britain to get married and have children. When Mary became queen in 1553, Davies fled to Switzerland. After the death of Mary in 1558 Davies returned to Britain. Two years later, Queen Elizabeth arranged for him to become Bishop of St. Asaph. Davies was a close friend of Queen Elizabeth's chief minister, Robert Cecil and became his main adviser on Welsh affairs. Davies also played an important role in the growth of Protestant ideas in Wales. In 1563 Richard Davies and his friend, William Salesbury, were given permission to translate the Bible into Welsh. The New Testament appeared in 1567, but following strong criticism of their work, Davies and Salesbury abandoned their plans to translate the Old Testament. Richard Davies died on 7th November, 1581.

William Davies was born in Caernarfonshire in about 1560. A Roman Catholic, Davies was educated in Rheims, France. He returned to Wales in 1585. Davies settled in Little Orme in Caernarfonshire where he conducted Roman Catholic services in secret. Davies also arranged the printing of Welsh translations of Catholic books. These were probably the first books ever to be printed in Wales. When Queen Elizabeth's ministers heard about Davies' activities they gave orders for his arrest. When the soldiers arrived at the cave where Davies had been hiding, they found a printing press and a considerable amount of Catholic literature. Davies was eventually arrested at Holyhead, where he was attempting to find a boat to take him to Ireland. Davies was found guilty of high treason and was hung, drawn and quartered on 21st July, 1593.

Robert Ferrar was born in Halifax, Yorkshire in about 1500. After studying at Cambridge University he became an Augustine monk at St. Mary's Priory, Oxford. In 1528 Ferrar became converted to the ideas of Martin Luther. Ferrar lost the right to preach when his strong Protestant beliefs became known. The situation changed when Edward VI became king and, in 1548, Ferrar was sent to Wales to convert people to Protestantism. Later that year he was appointed as Bishop of St David's. When, in 1549, priests were given the right to marry, Ferrar was one of the first members of the clergy to get married. Ferrar's decision to order the removal of church altars in his diocese made him unpopular with Catholics. They also disapproved of his sermons in support of a married clergy. On the death of Edward VI, a large number of Welsh Catholics appealed to Queen Mary to have the Bishop of St David's removed from office. Queen Mary ordered his arrest and in March, 1554 he was charged with breaking the vow of chastity. Ferrar, the father of two children, was found guilty and burnt at the stake on 30th March, 1555.

Elis Gruffydd was born in Gronant, Flintshire in about 1490. After being cheated out of twenty acres of land which he had owned in Gronant, he went to England where he found work as a servant in Sir Robert Wingfield's household in London. In 1523, Gruffydd accompanied Wingfield during a military campaign against France. By 1530 Gruffydd was back living in Flintshire. In about 1555 Gruffydd began work on *The Chronicle*. The book attempted to cover the history of England and Wales from the creation to the 1550s. In the later stages of the book, Gruffydd includes details of his own experiences. Elis Gruffydd died in about 1565.

William Herbert was born in 1501. William was the eldest son of Sir Richard Herbert of Ewyas, Herefordshire and Margaret Craddock of Swansea. As a young man he entered the service of Charles Somerset, Earl of Worcester. In 1527 William Herbert fled to France after killing a man in a fight. He eventually returned to England, where he married Anne Parr, the sister of Catherine, the sixth wife of Henry VIII. In 1542, Henry VIII gave his brother-in-law the estates of Wilton Abbey. The following year William Herbert was appointed governor of Aberystwyth. In 1549, William Herbert led an army of 2,000 Welshmen against farmers rebelling against enclosure. Afterwards he was rewarded with grants of land in Glamorgan, Monmouthshire and Breconshire. William Herbert was also awarded castles at Cardiff, Aberavon and Caerphilly. In 1550, Henry VIII appointed William to the post of President of the Council of Wales. The following year he was granted the title, the Earl of Pembroke. In 1553 the Earl of Pembroke arranged for his eldest son Henry to marry Catherine, the sister of Lady Jane Grey. On the death of Edward VI he was accused of being involved in the plot to make Lady Jane Grey queen of England and Wales. The Earl of Pembroke denied the charge and after he declared his support for Mary, he was released from custody. The Earl of Pembroke resumed office under Elizabeth and served her until his death at Hampton Court on 17th March, 1570.

Henry Herbert was born in 1534. Henry, the eldest son of the 1st Earl of Pembroke, was educated at Peterhouse, Cambridge, and at the age of nineteen married Catherine Grey, the sister of Lady Jane Grey. Henry was accused, along with his father, of being involved in the plot to make Lady Jane Grey queen of England and Wales. Henry Herbert demonstrated his loyalty to Queen Mary by joining her army fighting in France. On the death of his father in 1570, Henry became the 2nd Earl of Pembroke. Henry took a prominent role in the trial of Mary, Queen of Scots and in 1586 he was rewarded with the post of President of the Council of Wales. Henry Herbert, 2nd Earl of Pembroke, died on 9th January, 1601.

William Herbert was born on 8th April, 1580. William, the eldest son of the 2nd Earl of Pembroke, was educated at New College, Oxford and on the death of his father in 1601, became the 3rd Earl of Pembroke. Soon afterwards, he was arrested on the orders of Queen Elizabeth after it was discovered that he was the father of the child born to her Maid of Honour, Mary Fitton. When William refused to marry Mary Fitton, Elizabeth had him banished from court. Three years later, he married Mary Talbot, daughter of the Earl of Shrewsbury. The Earl of Pembroke was a talented poet and was a close friend of William Shakespeare. He was also interested in exploration and after visiting America helped to form the North West Passage Company. When Queen Elizabeth died in 1603, the Earl of Pembroke returned to court. In 1615 he was appointed James I's Lord Chamberlain. William Herbert died on 10th April, 1630.

Humphrey Llwyd was born in Denbigh in 1527. After graduating from Oxford University he became Lord Arundel's private physician. In 1563, Llwyd returned to Wales and became a doctor in Denbigh. For the next four years he also represented Denbigh in the House of Commons. Llwyd wrote several books, including *The Breviary of Britain* which featured one of the first known maps of Wales. Llwyd died on 31st August, 1568. During the last years of his life, Llwyd was working on a history of Wales but he died before he could finish the project. *The History of Cambria* was completed after his death by David Powell and published in 1584.

Rice Mansel came from a large land-owning family in Glamorgan. In 1512 he served in Henry VIII's army fighting in France. Mansel fought with distinction and afterwards became one of Henry VIII's advisers. When Henry VIII closed down the Welsh monasteries he offered Rice Mansel the Margam Abbey estates. A price of £2,482 was agreed and the money was paid in several instalments between 1540 and 1557. The Margam estates made Mansel the second largest landlord in Glamorgan. Mansel was one of Henry VIII's most valued commanders and, during the summer of 1545, he recruited over 2,000 men in Glamorgan to fight in the king's army against the French. After the death of Henry VIII, Mansel loyally served his son, Edward VI. Between 1551 and 1553 he was responsible for removing treasures from Glamorgan churches and sending them to the royal treasury. Two of Mansel's sons (Anthony and Edward) and two of his grandsons (Thomas and Robert) were members of parliament for Glamorgan. Rice Mansel died in 1559.

Thomas Myddelton was born at Denbigh Castle in 1560. He moved to London where he became a successful businessman. Eventually, Myddelton became a partner in the famous East India Company. By 1595, Myddelton was rich enough to purchase Chirk Castle. Two years later he was elected as member of parliament for Merioneth. In 1609, Thomas Myddelton and his brother, Hugh, financed the building of a 38 mile canal from Hertfordshire to Clerkenwell in London. Myddelton used some of his considerable wealth to pay for several puritan books to be published in the Welsh language. In 1630, Myddelton and another London merchant, Rowland Heylin, paid for the printing of a cheap edition of the Welsh Bible. Thomas Myddelton died in August, 1631.

William Morgan was born in Penmachno, Caernarfonshire in about 1540. William's father, John ap Morgan, a tenant farmer, could not afford to send his son away to school but, his landlord, Sir John Wynn, heard about William's intellectual abilities and arranged for him to be educated at Cambridge University. While he was at university, William Morgan was converted to Protestantism. After leaving university, William became vicar of Welshpool Church. In 1578 he moved to the church at Llanrhaeadr-ym-Mochnant in Denbighshire. Four years later Morgan began translating the Bible into Welsh. William Morgan's Welsh Bible was eventually published in 1588. Within a few months there was a Welsh Bible in every parish church in Wales. In 1595, William Morgan was elected Bishop of Llandaff. Six years later, Morgan moved to the better paid post of Bishop of St. Asaph. William Morgan died on 10th September, 1604.

George Owen was born in Henllys, Pembrokeshire in 1552. Like his father George became a lawyer in Pembrokeshire. For several years he was Vice Admiral of Pembrokeshire and in 1587 he was appointed Sheriff of the county. Owen was the author of several books, including the *Description of Wales* (1602) and *Description of Pembrokeshire* (1603). George Owen died in 1613.

William Salesbury was born in Llansannan, Denbighshire in about 1520. While studying at Oxford University he was converted to the Protestant faith. After leaving university he began work on collecting old Welsh proverbs, which were published under the title *Oll Syn Wyr Pen Kembero* in 1546. Salesbury believed strongly that the Welsh people should know their own language. To help them do this he published the first ever English and Welsh dictionary in 1547. Salesbury's next project was a Welsh translation of the Epistles and Gospels which was published in 1551 with the title, *Kynniver Llith a Ban*. When Mary became queen in 1553, Salesbury, a committed Protestant, went into hiding. His career prospects were much improved by the death of Mary in 1558. In 1563 Elizabeth gave permission for Salesbury to translate and print the first Welsh Bible. The book was published in 1567. Although he was helped by Richard Davies and Thomas Huett, Salesbury was responsible for the bulk of the translation. Salesbury was stung by the criticisms that were made of his work and as a result, produced no further translations. William Salesbury died in 1600.

William Somerset was born at Raglan Castle in 1526. The eldest son of Henry, 2nd Earl of Worcester, William was appointed principal esquire to Henry VIII in 1544. On the death of his father in 1549, William became the 3rd Earl of Worcester. As well as inheriting the family estates, William also acquired the land previous owned by Tintern Abbey. Although William retained his Roman Catholic beliefs, he loyally served Edward VI and Queen Elizabeth. In 1588 he raised a force to help defend the Welsh coast against the threatened invasion from Spain. William Somerset, 3rd Earl of Worcester died at Raglan Castle on 22nd February, 1588.

Henry Tudor was born at Pembroke Castle on 28th January, 1457. Henry's mother, Margaret Beaufort, was only 13 years old when he was born. Henry's father, Edmund Tudor, Earl of Richmond had recently died and his uncle, Jasper Tudor, became his guardian. During the War of the Roses, the Tudor family supported the Lancastrians. In 1468, William Herbert, a Yorkist commander, took Henry prisoner when he captured Pembroke Castle. Jasper Tudor obtained his release, but on the death of Henry VI in 1471, the two men were forced to flee to France. In 1485, Henry and Jasper returned to Wales and with the help of Welsh soldiers were able to defeat Richard III. The following year, Henry VII married Elizabeth of York and thereby uniting the two families. Henry VII died in 1509.

Jasper Tudor was born in Anglesey in about 1431. He was knighted by his half-brother, Henry VI on 25 December, 1449. Jasper Tudor was one of Henry VI's senior commanders during the War of the Roses. However, after being defeated by the Yorkist army at Harlech, he was forced to flee to France. In 1485, Jasper returned to Wales with Henry Tudor. After Henry became king in 1485 he appointed Jasper Tudor as Chief Justice of Wales. Jasper Tudor died on 21st December, 1495.